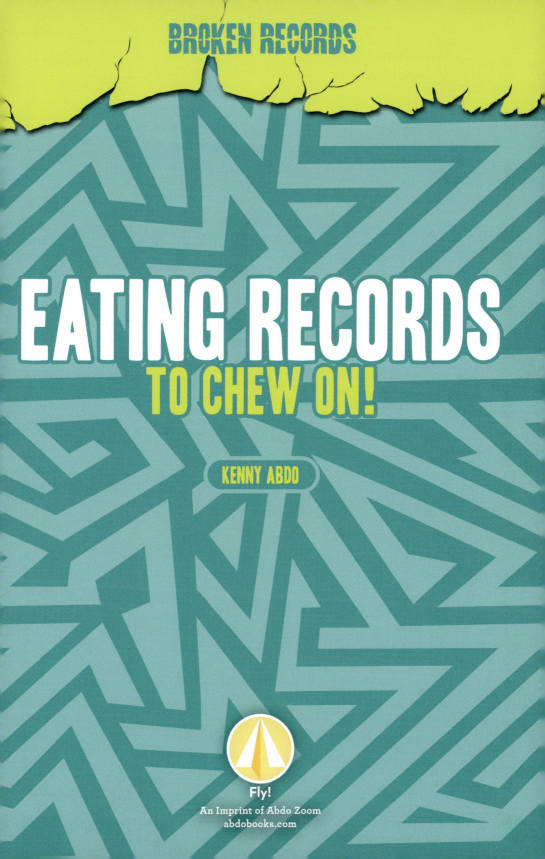

## abdobooks.com

Published by Abdo Zoom, a division of ABDO, P.O. Box 398166, Minneapolis, Minnesota 55439. Copyright © 2024 by Abdo Consulting Group, Inc. International copyrights reserved in all countries. No part of this book may be reproduced in any form without written permission from the publisher. Fly!™ is a trademark and logo of Abdo Zoom.

Printed in the United States of America, North Mankato, Minnesota.
052023
092023

THIS BOOK CONTAINS RECYCLED MATERIALS

Photo Credits: Alamy, AP Images, Getty Images, Shutterstock
Production Contributors: Kenny Abdo, Jennie Forsberg, Grace Hansen
Design Contributors: Candice Keimig, Neil Klinepier, Laura Graphenteen

**Library of Congress Control Number: 2022946931**

**Publisher's Cataloging-in-Publication Data**

Names: Abdo, Kenny, author.
Title: Eating records to chew on! / by Kenny Abdo
Description: Minneapolis, Minnesota : Abdo Zoom, 2024 | Series: Broken records | Includes online resources and index.
Identifiers: ISBN 9781098281397 (lib. bdg.) | ISBN 9781098282097 (ebook) | ISBN 9781098282448 (Read-to-me ebook)
Subjects: LCSH: Records--Juvenile literature. | History--Juvenile literature. | Eating contests--Juvenile literature.
Classification: DDC 032.02--dc23

# TABLE OF CONTENTS

Eating Records .................. 4

Broken Records ................. 8

For the Record ................. 20

Glossary ...................... 22

Online Resources .............. 23

Index ......................... 24

# EATING RECORDS

Everybody loves food. But some people love it so much, they leave the table with world records and no leftovers!

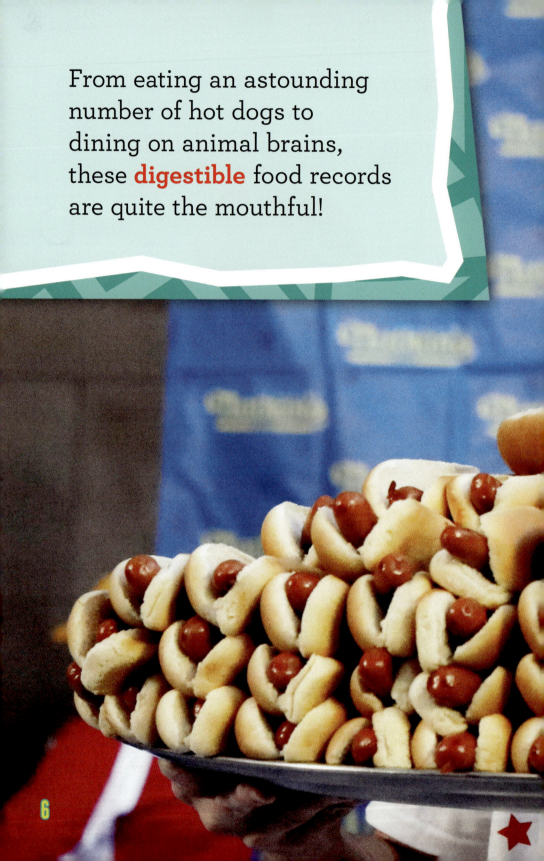

From eating an astounding number of hot dogs to dining on animal brains, these **digestible** food records are quite the mouthful!

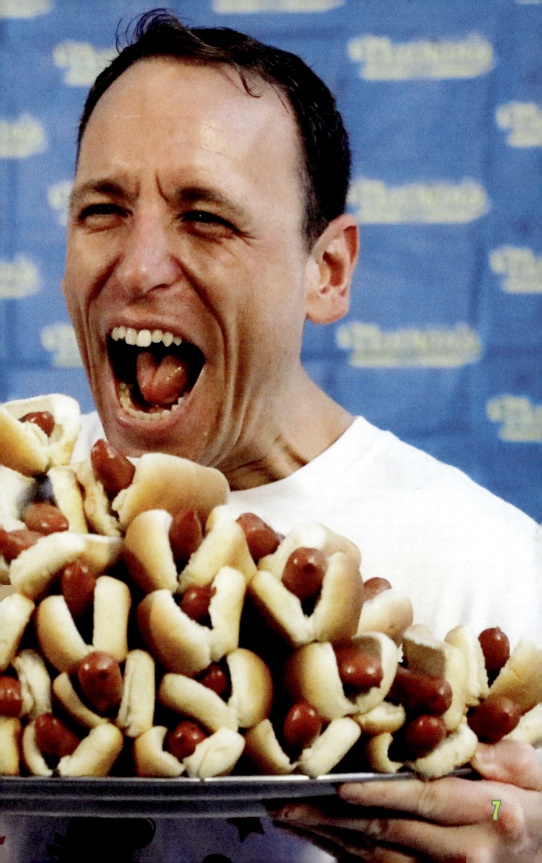

# BROKEN RECORDS

From 1965 to 1966, Angus Barbieri **fasted** for 382 days. He had only soda water, coffee, tea, and vitamins. Barbieri lost 276 lbs (125 kg), earning the **Guinness World Record** for longest fast without solid food. To not **encourage** longer periods without eating, Guinness no longer awards records for fasting.

In 2002, **competitive eater** Takeru Kobayashi gobbled up 57 cow brains in just 15 minutes. With an overall weight of 18 lbs (8 kgs) eaten, Kobayashi had one smart meal!

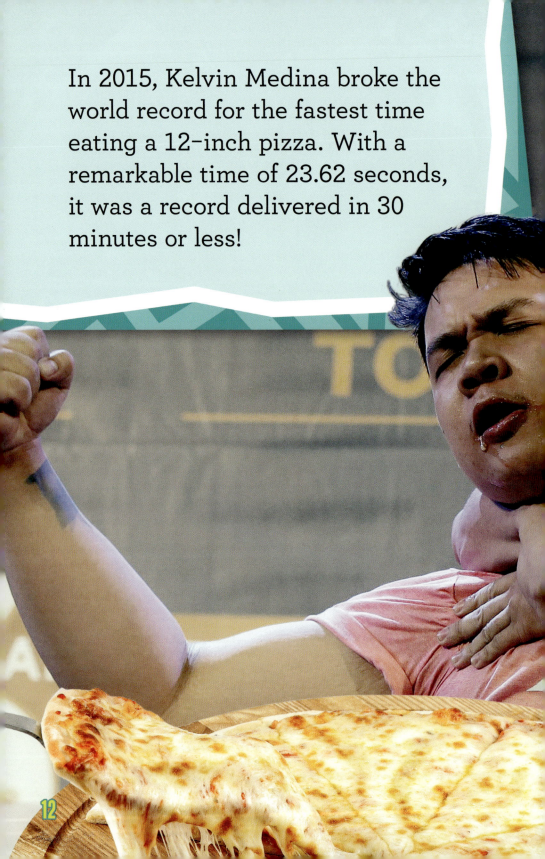

In 2015, Kelvin Medina broke the world record for the fastest time eating a 12-inch pizza. With a remarkable time of 23.62 seconds, it was a record delivered in 30 minutes or less!

Back in 2017, Matt Stonie took down 255 Peeps in just five minutes. He broke his record from the previous year of eating 200 of the little marshmallow birds! Stonie got a rush from the record and the sugar!

No one outmatches Joey Chestnut when it comes to eating hot dogs. In 2020, he broke his own world record by eating 75 dogs in just 10 minutes! Frankly, it was an impressive **feat**.

Miki Sudo holds an incredible amount of eating records. In 2022, she took the **Guinness World Record** for eating a whole burrito in 31.47 seconds! It is a record that is all it's wrapped up to be!

# FOR THE RECORD

Eating is an important part of life. For those who do it competitively, landing a record can be quite fulfilling. It can be stomach filling, too!

# GLOSSARY

**competitive eater** – a person who competes against others to eat large amounts of food in a short period of time.

**digestible** – easy to understand or follow.

**encourage** – to give approval to.

**fast** – to stop eating food completely for a certain amount of time.

**feat** – an achievement that requires a lot of skill or strength.

**Guinness World Record** – an award given to those who have broken a record never achieved before.

# ONLINE RESOURCES

To learn more about eating records, please visit **abdobooklinks.com** or scan this QR code. These links are routinely monitored and updated to provide the most current information available.

# INDEX

Barbieri, Angus 9

Chestnut, Joey 17

Guinness World Record (award) 9

Kobayashi, Takeru 11

Medina, Kelvin 12

Peeps (candy) 15

speed 12, 15, 17, 19

Stonie, Matt 15

Sudo, Miki 19

weight 9, 11